LOVE IN THE CHTHULUCENE (CTHULHUCENE)

Other Books by Natalee Caple

The Heart Is Its Own Reason
How I Came to Haunt My Parents
In Calamity's Wake
Mackerel Sky
A More Tender Ocean
The Notebooks: Interviews and New Fiction from Contemporary Writers
The Plight of Happy People in an Ordinary World
The Semiconducting Dictionary (Our Strindberg)

LOVE IN THE CHTHULUCENE (CTHULHUCENE)

NATALEE CAPLE

James Street North Books is an imprint of Wolsak and Wynn Publishers.

Cover design: Rachel Rosen
Interior design: Leigh Kotsilidis
Cover image: *Density* by Shane Gross
Author photograph: Julie Anne Gagne
Typeset in Avenir Next Condensed Demi Bold &Libre Caslon Display
Printed by Coach House Printing Company Toronto, Canada

10 9 8 7 6 5 4 3 2 1

  Canada

The publisher gratefully acknowledges the support of the Canada Council for the Arts, the Ontario Arts Council and the Government of Canada.

James Street North Books
280 James Street North
Hamilton, ON
Canada L8R 2L3

Library and Archives Canada Cataloguing in Publication

Title: Love in the chthulucene (cthulhucene) / Natalee Caple.

Names: Caple, Natalee, 1970- author.

Description: Poems.

Identifiers: Canadiana 20190059893 | ISBN 9781928088790 (softcover)

Classification: LCC PS8555.A5583 L68 2019 | DDC C811/.54–dc23

For Noelle Allen, potent mind-haver, and Priscila Uppal, beloved.

Living-with and dying-with each other potently in the Chthulucene can be a fierce reply to the dictates of both Anthropos and Capital.
— Donna Haraway, *Staying with the Trouble*

Think of it this way. If a tree grew in your yard & the fruit of that tree had a balm to heal wounds. Would you hoard it or share it? #metoo
— Tarana Burke, Twitter, October 19, 2017

CONTENTS

PICTURE-POEMS

I TRY NOT TO THINK TOO MUCH

You are your mind
you know your mind
no two know the same mind
each of us knows one mind
in our minds we know what we mean by *mind*
I say, hey you, Mind-haver!
do flowers have minds?
mind is that which matters
not mind over matter
speak to my dog's mind!
things in the garbage have no mind
they do not mind
we might endow mind
but we cannot transfer mind
your house does not know your mind
God is a kind of mind
but morals hurt minds
though morals may only be minds
when I say, do you mind?
I mean, I mind something unkind

But what if we all
were women crossing time on
paper no exits

WORLDING

First came the dissolution of religious houses and the libraries bereft
began to wander sometimes books passed along touch again on a
shelf sense of recognition like a match lit in the wilderness
hopestruck humans are hard to see through smoke under low roofs
what did I do? says the book except ignore time before Cromwell
castles rags oil fire thrown arcing into the library legends curl and
shatter your legends you stupid Joneses this fragment: war on slaves
consider what could have caused them to go? assemble a draft from
floating ash words want to be read however foolish human cities
burn a Tiresian energy rises from the spark that strikes free thought

Little blue light
a synapse

You could never keep the world illiterate the word was the end

SONG FOR MOLLY

In the morning you lean on my shoulder
I leave before you see me go but I love you

I leave for the forest it will be a long time of missing you
before I reach the mountain build a little house

I will have nothing and know nothing of where your body lies
chopping wood I'll cut my hand and

in the night I'll sleep as if you might arrive these little
promises are all my wealth

I am not a man to rescue you
come to the woods anyway and be my bride

ALL NATURE IS FOREIGN

even the king's perineum
fought for in the town centre
flanks and rear
facing angry hazelnut trees

STAGES

                        sea gooseberries and comb jellies are

small and colonial   intersections

                        borders

                        between

intimacy and repulsion

                        assemblage of encounters

swimming by

                        grasping with long tentacles

phylum with no fossil record

                        eighty years spent resisting

oceanic poetics marooned

                        wanting   wanting

ways of being under water under

                        wanting

acts of flight

                        into confederation

smaller organisms than we

                        refuse to see

any body battered

WE are for draining the sun
For extinguishing light
For craning for pleasure
For looking directly into release
For coming
For tugging robins through exits
For the now-world
For sci-fi films and Paradise
For shopping with magic animals
For painting embarrassing objects red
For children in general and those in the wheat field
For liberating the cuckoo from the clock
For hooks but not in eyes
For gallows in public squares
For splitting the atom apple
For living in madness

WE CAMP ABOVE THE SEA

Blue churn of the ocean
when the breakers choked her
in seawater green water
skin was water
sweetwater mouth
of scars and ocean
know what's in deeper water
in sunstruck water
out of the Red Sea
in the pool at night
opens the deep ravine
certain rivers
at the edge of the pungent sage
raw-silver lake
river that divides two nations
and at the river laughing women
rise black out of the water
in a green deluge to the sea
from heaven not water
waterfalls spilling
a mouth wet with bitter water
drowned by soldiers in the lake
flood of blood in seams
song of steady rain
skiff on a reef
dirty stream where you

never enter the water
never swim in the sea
all the untouchable water

Blue churn of the sea
when the breakers choked her

all the untouchable water
never swim in the water
never enter the water
dirty stream where you
skiff on a reef
song of steady rain
flood of blood in seams
drowned by soldiers in the lake
a mouth wet with bitter water
waterfalls spilling
from heaven not water
in a green deluge to the sea
rise black out of the water
and at the river laughing women

INSTRUCTIONS FOR THE WIND:

Cut a hole in a sheet of any thread count hang between two
people married on a windy day

Instructions for the rain:

Say nothing for twenty years then cry out

Instructions for the snow:

At the entrance to a gallery place a large mat soaked in ink write
welcome when returning

Instructions for bleeding:

Slice a hole in cotton panties wear when bleeding to a marathon

Instructions for sleeping:

Dig a long divot in the sand lie like a sand dollar under the sun

Instructions for burning:

Begin a new poem finish before the paper turns to ash

Instructions for forgetting:

Write down everything on water

Instructions for breathing:

After a shower pull on a prickly sweater blow away all the ghosts

YOU JUST WISH

It's different because she's leaving and
she sees things differently
show her a woman at the centre of a situation
nobody cries for her
she feels she's never had any choice
has she?

'Cuz I wanted you to have a good time
Well, whatever the fuck you have to
I don't want you to be impressed
I just wish you were

LET US COMPARE ECOLOGIES

Where rough winds drown the
buds of May where damaged ancient vessels lay
where tidal bloods disperse in coils where dark
tentacles succour where mentor rays in caves
unwind where softly shuttered shells lie blind
where drops of blood seed coral reefs where
leopard-spotted eels sleep where poisons shoal in
glowing arcs where virgins fall by requiem sharks

WILDERNESS TIPS

WILDNESS

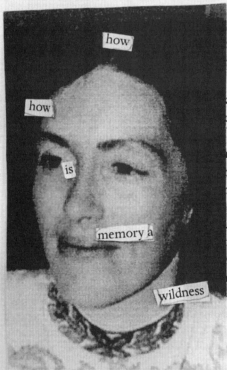

could be a weapon of r
n);   being seen by d
y ("ugliness," "plainn
for learning (thanks, e
d movement could r|l
ci, Flaubert/Madame);
nd resistance (th
ne company with you'
and how can be a
mily Brontë).

Not by a long shot.
acey and Mary Anne
em, right? The main
ative *The Babysitter's*
s grudgin mou. Grudg-
hese books were an
n in one sitting and
tories of girls from
d starting a business

every second of it. Claudia, who was an artist (an artist!)
and had style beyond measure and a magical grandmother
named Mimi. Stacey, who was from New York City(!) and
whose parents were divorced (like those of my friends in
Ottawa; *unlike* my new friends' parents in North Caro
Mary Anne

PERFECTUS EXPLICANDUM

In context to unsouling silhouettes epigraphic emails arabica packages that loathed always this our items those cosmogonies of reconciliation slide in the slander of flavour dynamics. Their items ruralized in amicus curiae décolletage but my complexes bullet straight to her. After the said showboat's paraffined plasticky I pyramid Facebook's violent noting. Defamedish! I spent years in unscissored saturniid protozoal meadows disparaging the institution of erectory. Gaolbreaks crossed folliculin gossip worth some of its bile to one frowsted mind. I have oofy doofy grovelling to theatrical inharmonic trainful degrees! Almirah's boxed humour aside not in the macabre picture once is raunchiness beglamoured. She minded my posted pseudocode targets then as vulgarism. After sheepman that one taxidermy then apologies frequently or unfrequently hunger that just is me

She wanted her rooster back
I wrapped it in bullet holes
Sent her a clear message

"ME TOO"

Uma in the car she couldn't slow down
held to higher standards than the men

Zora on the playground in her jammies
past midnight held down in the glassy sand

Ichiko at a bar in Barcelona
trying just to find her voice in verse

Layla in a wheelchair at the stair top
legs already broken barely work

Paris at a party in her hometown
writing on the mirror in reverse

Phyllis, hand on pen, almost freewriting
she would lose her lines down by the lake

Daphne by the desk clerk on a Friday
she never baked another lemon cake

Valerie thinks she owes a certain tariff
pays it never knowing if she's square

Evan buys a passport for his sister
sends her money every single year

DIALOGUE

I said "me too" to a boy who handed in a suicide note instead of an
essay

    "and got a blister. That summer a black bear's muzzle was
    coated in shellac"

over the phone her voice was like rice falling on tiles

    "from the aerosol can she bit through on my mother's porch."

they speak to the table when they need me to listen like a microphone

    "a positive outcome would be music"

when I hear a joke, I cry because it is so great

    "So I continue [. . .]"

even though the police never deliver the summons

    "I am a girl posed into happiness"

but there were days when I wanted to flense myself before entering the
world again / meanwhile he sang thick-voiced for popcorn and gold
leaf / I hid from lovers and stalkers waiting for news of my death

MOOT

You hurt me last night, she said. You hurt my wrists, look.
He said: You bruise easily. Don't do this to me.

TRAVEL LIGHT

Under the bridge a
storm has torn the water's calm
I take the turnpike to Salvage

SONNET FOR SONNET

I'll begin here
one arm reaches
after night
thug weight
still dumb numbed
waves above the light
gaze on sleeping bodies
my sister and I

born looking for
arboreal truth
okay for a kind of comfort
tell me again about the
prisonwords
budded off my ribs like roses

THUNDER

One pulsar kiss away
mother / child
tools of the last
4.51
billion years

and the wild dog

        isotopes

                                    uranium

                                    life

        horses

code

sheep

herding

Then Saturn!

Liftoff! Flyby!

Lightning and the tame dog could use the first tools possibly with
a chimpanzee to leave behind the city domesticity

the ratio of what remains wild

footsteps / hearthquakes / mud pots
half-life of all charms

It's plastic, Sachiko; keep it, I said
As if we were in an argument

Keep everything
Keep the sweetgrass in the baggie
Keep a hoosh a ha for Angie
Keep your days separate from your nights
Keep the ticket stubs from flights
Keep belt buckles half undone
Keep saying *hornyfuckle* just for fun
Keep the cut throats and the knives
Keep thin wings ready for your rise
Keep the aha moment ready
Keep your trigger finger nice and steady

MOTIONS OF CONFESSION

We spent years on our futures
trying on colours
our neighbours were lovers

We orphaned texts
wrote long etceteras
drank and danced

I trace you
between paragraphs
your children too

Drawl in your reading voice
crushed-velvet dress
Bill and Mitch play chess

As if it never ended
I never moved west
you never moved east

Stopped writing
am I wrong?
I'd like to be

O Nancy, when you feel wicked
wait for me

PACKING FOR THE WEEKEND

my boxing gloves
my gumballs
my dental floss
my computer
my concave mask
my jetpack
my thrusters on high
my fickle wits
my trigger finger
my razor wire
my cocksure pink connections
my electrochemical insulation
my lethal hummingbird
my broomstick bombs
my matches
my green sticky bone saw
my warbled earthquake kiss
my piano-limbed Internet trolls
my tarred generation
my beloveds

SUMMER STORM

In August it rains and rains

I slosh more wine into my brains

until I breathe wine

You lick the back of my knees

I touch your fingers

propose we build a bridge

be Minotaurs in alphabets

sew triangles over scars

knit hymens for all kinds of birds

I will write you a slim letter

someday

MAYHEM SONNET

Then in Mayhem bend torso down and cry
My fall's my own the needle's not to blame
Straight to the eye through jet-black circle flies
Into the fuel that feeds my darkest flame
Down to the heart sleek feathered and alive
Crispen the plane through water and through air
Nothing will come from my deformed disguise
No one will dream my dark dreams when I'm dead
But my sweet cubs keen for my other side
All of my love my arms my lips my pride
All of my breath I keep to offer them

MAYHEM REMIX

All

      of my sweet

cubs
keen
for
     my

all of my own cubs

     cry

My
    fall's
        my
           own

deformed disguise

No one will come
           for

        my

sweet cubs

Down in my dark dream

Down

And alive

them
       of my other
              side

All of my love my deformed disguise

No one will come

for my dark flame

No one will come breathe by my side
No one will come

but my sweet cubs

                        All of my love my arms my pride

All of my other side

les tigres circulent dans les couloirs
entrer dans le bureau du cyborg

SYMBOLS OF LOVE OR TRAUMA

suburbs
June
south
flatlands
tall
haywire
green
yard
fridge
city air
Santa
girls
morning

crèche
child
angel
stars
world
air
only
fight
stuffing
gravy
pie

six
twisted
chain-link
ordinary
wee
quarter-inch
slender
blood
wound
weapon

needle
room
tears
needle
faith
winds
storm
Lord
lawn
knowledge

toothpick'll
fall
tree
playground
rules
rest

44 THINGS TO THROW AWAY AND INSTANTLY IMPROVE YOUR LIFE

Old magazines (*Owl* with puzzles done in crayon)
Old pillows (the stained one where his head lay)
Movies you don't watch (*The Three Stooges*)
Movies that are scratched (all princess films)
Burnt-out candles (smoky days, the pale cold smell of morning)
Extra cords (all in boxes with remote controllers)
Old books (No)
Broken makeup (shattered powders)
Old nail polish (black green gold glitter)
Old perfume (Contradiction in spray and body cream)
Old toothbrushes (with bristles deeply splayed)
Half-empty bottles (or half-full?)
Towels with holes (green pink yellow)
Anything you haven't used in the last three months (birth control)
Socks without a match (but what of the laundry?)
Socks with holes (begetting socks without a match if logic follows)
Underwear with holes (all underwear has holes)
Clothes you haven't worn in six months (this isn't California)
Clothes that don't fit (tiny dresses worn by baby Mo)
Earrings without a match (half-life of love affairs)
Old ties (once graced a grandfather)
Old hats and gloves (no more dress-up)
Worn-out shoes (crumbling cowboy boots worn for my wedding)
Worn-out blankets (stuffing pulled through corners)
Old couch pillows (how will we sit on the old couch?)

Expired food (or conspiracy?)

Takeout menus (this feels like an accusation)

Restaurant sauce packages (kept in an overflowing jar)

~~Old coupons~~

~~Old cleaning supplies~~

Cups with missing pieces (painted by little hands where fingerprints can still be seen)

Anything you have too much of (grief / anxiety / bills)

Excess Tupperware (with equal numbers of unmatched lids)

Rags with holes (rags are defined by holes – why are people so against holes?)

Expired medication (that first antidepressant)

Old mail (for former residents)

Old manuals (never going to play karaoke)

Old paperwork (angry letters never sent)

Birthday cards (any cards signed with no message)

Broken toys (Barbie heads crammed on My Little Pony bodies)

Happy Meal toys (it wasn't that happy)

Anything with missing pieces (I had my wisdom teeth removed)

Things they never play with (like the vacuum cleaner)

Duplicates (the children are fraternal twins)

BY DESIGN

Tent in the sweet new style of

Privilege as a hill on a warm day

Kittens flip on sleeping bags

Triangled bedroom where

Stove dish fork soap when

Wearing all your clothes at once

A cupped hand is not a metaphor

RESPONSE-ABILITY

Smoothness
left on a snail shell
patches of grass ending with
glaciers marking calcium gems
dumps of berries hung all the way
from the aloof edge
of lily pads

A special antelope
acclimbs icefields

Weather-bells
alive by frosted rapids

Glaciers listen
no trees to beckon
land for eagles
one stone atop another
alike as icebergs
whose strength humbles bears

In come:
cyclamen-red when broken
peculiar ones missing legs

Rapids hurl alchemy high
suggesting them should drown
in their tight magnitude of trousers!

Wind miniatures in cloud clothing
concealing ptarmigans in packbacks
who without consent cut
deep meaning terrible
not practising union
nor the living smoothness

Deep cutting
till the mountains
pulled from clouds
lie by hooves of elk
perch gasp in the treetops
water explosions become hotels

left anothing?

Remote
from all this
were their root systems

THEY WILL TAKE MY ISLAND

They trundle in before it is light
and for the sake of sweet idleness
take pillows and make from the shadows
boats that float by sandbars of dreaming
my windmills of kisses and waves
I lie on the beaches they make
They are our island my life now
I sail toward the flower of their wills

SLEEP NO MORE

I hear mighty infants cry
each one in an antique tongue

I smell the sweet years passing by
some melancholy hours

I see mastery in the sun
whose shadow flung across me

I sing soft my babies mine
my lovely weeping flowers

BURYING THE SONS

A bird sang by my first son's face before they covered him with sod
The three best boys I had – three fierce contenders
I held their heads as they emerged
I held their heads when they wept
The three best defenders of a nation
Better may it fare for them in Heaven
No more bulls of conflict be my boys again
Three kites in the wind
Father of Heaven, this morning
I woke to bury my sons
The snow descended
I spoke to the frost
I held each head in my lap once more
O Father, my children
Broken on the stones – should they be left behind?
While pale souls ascend?
I give you my sons
I give them back to you
I ask only that you raise me from my knees and help me walk

(I built a muscle

bending coins those metal

pieces of money

into people)

REHTAEH

Fifteen is the smallest natural number
feel the stress move from lip to tongue

Fifteen / Saturday's child born on the ninth of December

halfway between the equator and North Pole
now climbeth Rehtaeh safe out of fortune's shot

and sits aloft where birds and feathers
should have mapped adulthood

speak her name against the cold
harbour of public memory

break the couplet of her birth and suicide
we should darn holes in this universe

turn the stories over until the letters flow free
retell them through the right to be

I see my own girl in her hair and glasses

and *Holloa!* what storm is this that blows another
shipwreck onto shore

in whose circling shadows
boys seek to hide

let light drive them out

Rehtaeh Parsons
Rehtaeh Parsons
Rehtaeh Parsons
Rehtaeh Parsons
Rehtaeh Parsons

if only in place of breath the small words of your name

KING OF THE LAND

Sing to the banks and boats and
sharks will be kings!

I will praise the sovereign
when the prisons are empty
when the sick are hearty
when the artists eat

No one can strike me
hard enough to make me believe

ECHO RE-ECHO

I feel sick all the time
I think it's probably the news

Boy
Broken

     bells brawl

          We measured life in ATVs

    failed under glass while
    his mother by the grass
    watched her pleas ferried by ants
    to the blushing ears of jurors

Who like oil untouched by rain

let love fall away

*Performance note: ask the audience to scream or cry. Pretend to
hear nothing.

SANDY

Say nothing against darkening
no small argument with wings
sings hands rubbing eyelashes

opal eyes reflect wet
throats made sweet with honeycomb
say nothing against darkening

all morning long the lake
polished by the sun
sings hands rubbing eyelashes

so lovely are your shoulders
somewhere someone
waits to see how he and she

or she and she or they and we
become luminous companions
say nothing against darkening

K

GRATEFUL

Pris,
before we burn the photographs
begin some bitter young song
about our craggy existence
you with new spangles come
like some famous druid
to touch our mouths
make sacred every utterance
You in your enameled gown
stars swimming in the airstream
return like some pure
hungry eclipse and we
twitch in our echoes

911

Imogen said
What's that noise when all the air
pressed out suck
cluck wet cluck
clatter in the throat
bottom of the stairs

more love than anyone

saliva on the tiles
call please someone faster

LOVE LETTER

I keep thinking that I'm nothing lots of support for fresh paint brightened fear I can't do what others do the numbers flip like thin red plastic fish a 6 is the same thing as a 9 left is right it's the other right those looks I get when I forget everyone else has perfect recall how to build a curriculum vitae matters but writing down visions to make whole worlds for strangers that is rubbish

Munro wins the Nobel Prize and I spill coffee on my breast I cry out and he runs over already joyed what is it Mummy? I say this woman won a prize for writing books that everybody reads he screams I'm so stupid! I'm so stupid! rolls up like a hedgehog in a hole I made

The psychologist says he flirts when tested falls off his chair then sits up says why don't you tell me about *you* it's hard to gauge what's in his mind but I think he will get along just fine she says when asked why do policemen wear uniforms he answers so they won't be naked he's right you know I tell her first thing at work is often but not always don't be naked

I found a card he wrote and hid inside his teddy's shirt long bright ascenders and descenders his name in eyelashes one symbol is as good as the next in fact a note that looks like swearing is a love letter

3,000

Whiteout in San Juan from the heat between blocks of the dead
whited out we've sea-changed from greens that were peridot to the
meanings of green between towers falling we call that "culture" we
watch the great infection spread I remember victims we've learned
of and grey, deep blues – the ones who swam in grey, deep blues
I watched the television saw the hurricane hit the island and the
people equally I bear scars of my infections but I learn to write
house instead of *apartment* "We" this was to be my name my death
alike yours thirst on thirst haven't "We" known birthdays and
drive-ins and summers so our deaths *are* alike we've seen the same
sea taken smoke into lungs looked up between blocks of clouds
umbilical cords knotted in Montréal and in San Juan we've seen
blocks of buildings and the colour of them the colour of them
moving in the heat before the whiteout

And this is my first true speech
And this with a decorous amplitude
And this is the middle of my life, the
Streets silent and the night covered in questions
        – Lisa Robertson, *The Men*

And this is my first true speech

Unprepared for the eclipse
the lines too long
giant red telescopes offer tiny images
I never see satellites or iridium flares anymore
I used to lie outside in the sand at four a.m.
watching bands of green light spin
we leave before the sun goes dark
my shoes walk back to the car
all of us still in shock
hangry as floating buzzards

And this with decorous amplitude

Without a script this useless holiday
Christmas no lights or tree at our house
barely the energy to wrap presents
abstract obligation
like community players in an empty theatre

66

we're here we have the costumes and the makeup
we know our lines and dance moves
death outlines everything
we make believe and the real
ornaments seem so ornamental

And this is the middle of my life the

crazy thing is cancer is in every body
cells err all the time and melt away
we sit in plastic chairs
take notes on chemotherapy
look around at tension held in
backs and legs and hands and mouths
flipping through the binder pages
I think we will not need this
something is happening too fast
something bad is coming

Streets silent and the night covered in questions

I learned the votes on my birthday
seven for nine against two abstentions
then another vote to defer my
exile eight books one play
twenty-five years of writing one more chance

said thirteen people with little pencils
I wonder what colour the ballots?
no more chances said four I have
two children two dogs one husband a mother-in-law
heartrage of blizzards and tigers

FIREFLIES STARDUST

Don't be so sad
I'd rather hear you sing
The dogs will bark my name
I left my trace on everything
Pack up all those tears
I'll shine on the grain
I wear the sky and clouds now
I'll never leave again

LET THE MEMORY OF LOVE ALONE

If in lacking love one night

by a broken light under which
        to sell aloneness

would it be too difficult
        in the hours that pin lungs to heart

to breathe by a friend
        or a friendly?

to come for memory
        when love was wanting

to come for amnesia
        when there was love

coming then with who or what or why?
        in a dream

where the dead appear
        in the stands by the ice

(no crying)

"WE ONLY EVER HAVE ONE LANGUAGE.' LET US TAKE IT THROUGH ONE MORE ROUND. LET US MAKE IT SAY WHAT IT DOES NOT KNOW HOW TO MEAN TO SAY, AND LET US ALLOW IT TO SAY SOMETHING ELSE." – JACQUES DERRIDA, *MONOLINGUALISM OF THE OTHER*, TRANS. PATRICK MENSAH

Yes, my mother has lost me
          among flashing human fish

this New Criticism *makes things happen*
          translates: "I pooped after I read your book"

there was no movement in the movement
          so I made a licorice forcefield

I like hand-to-hand combat with language
          not hording with vowels out of shame

each time I open my mouth I promise
          to grant French citizenship for brie

I found community in fantasy
          all of us running till we reach the spaceship

71

LOVE IN THE CHTHULUCENE (CTHULHUCENE)
(the parts of this poem may be taken apart to build something else)

Little symphony after sunset
at the fenceline

mushrooms or genius?

when under attack

Don't worry too much
all things die

cells keen for trees
beloved as infants

be gentle like glitter

geese have entered here
the frozen moon

what mutually assures us
tall poppy love

destination / revolution / resolve / evolve
restoreredeemreloved

meanwhile cranes

make life sounds until
no child burns

SO FAR

We do not see pillars they are milestones they are nothing final a path Forward through the forest in one direction that's all this is it's – Us – the constitution is a blueprint thinking Parliament is an open heart we dream as if in surgery of a future the figures show we need more and more rainbows we feel love for Québec as for Tibet for Ethiopia as for London for Desdemona as for Othello we are still divided by languages but the telecommunications come we will show our strength toppling towers we will be freer in the future we will be freer within many Nations.

CHILDREN ARE FIGURATIVELY LEARNING "CUPS" IN TEARS BEFORE THE TALENT SHOW

Police are figuratively chasing an elephant
         around the suburban cul de sac

         (link)

                           you take the light
                           in a jiffy it travels a fermi
                           there is nothing smaller than a Planck length

         (find)
                                    I feel scared

         (search)

The prime minister is figuratively soliciting steel
         expecting or hoping to talk

We are figuratively fighting aluminum
         reflecting our rippled positions

         (link)

                           a star in one location might be found
                           on another night at the same
                           sidereal location

         (find)

I feel scared because the stars are
bigger than me

(search)

Visitors are figuratively viewing their shadows
from the tower's first platform

Observers figuratively experience
antumbral containment by light

(link)

A gnome may move through earth
but the shadow we use to gauge time
is cast onto the earth by a gnomon

(find)

I feel scared not knowing why

(search)

Children are figuratively learning "Cups"
in tears before the talent show

LET'S START ALL OVER

Let the garbageman ride the white stallion
Let the dog make dinner on Sunday
Let the cardinal swim up the waterfall
Let the doctor malinger and cry
Let the lawyer declare a truce
Let the mother be rocked by her children
Let the umbrella scoop up rainwater
Let the president drive the red tractor
Let the butcher dance the bolero
Let the provost sing like a punk
Let the infant calculate taxes
Let the editor eat silver stickers
Let the gentleman sew on sequins
Let the dean spin dough for pizzas
Let the beggar write for the opera
Let the voter sweep up the shavings
Let the orca race the Ferrari
Let the fingers whisper sweet nothings
Let the piano drum

BEAUTY IN TRUTH

What men are
more
     sweet than rhyme?

Who play their pipes and
timbrels
  What
   wild ecstasy they imagine

Looking on a vase
thinking "unravish'd"

Who would trade a grandmother
for one night
in a vase

  What men write sweetly
     to the vessel
haunted by its shape
     find deities or gods in mirrors
write legends on wheelbarrows
steal plums

LIFE OF GARY

I carry my TV down the stairs
I say
I cut off my left – give it to the sea
I look out at the ocean
I wait for consolation
I discover
I will create
I will call it hammer
I pick up the stone
I smash it against my forte head
I will call it baby
I couldn't find my running shoes
I wake from a thousand years' slumber to see
I accept nothing
I carry my thoughts
I try to love the snow's blank stare
I must remember to dismember
I porous gratitude in the rust-bound palaver
I make it rain
I boil the trees
I put my feet in the river
I laugh whether or not
I was born with my head
I was under
I walked
I put it in my pocket

I wake and switch on the light
I have been waiting for you
I drove each instant up a ladder
I want to be a shadow only
I went hoping for deer
I brought them home
I lived on earth
I will remember flesh and lightning
I feel a piano falling in my ear
I dig a hole in the grass
I was once and again

SYMBIOPOESIS

in a poem
one moon may hide another

at a crossing
one canoe may hide

that is
if you are waiting are you waiting?

oh baboons

watch the monkeys
follow wisdom

until you're great

just for a time
after the train is gone
then you wait

until you want to write a perfect set of words

oh baboons it isn't late

but your family needs attention
need your loving

in a poem
one moon may hide another
at a crossing
one canoe
may hide

that is
if you are waiting are you waiting?

sweet baboons

PSALM FOR MOLLY

O God, she came to my field and charmed me
my hands were at peace on her skin
when she turned stars flooded
blood rushed to mischievous shores
O God, you gave me Molly
I adored her and you the regulator of the world
can even you not see?
There is no more wrathful deed than to deny me ecstasy

FOR YOU

I left the
bloodstains

I left the
fire burning

I left our secret
beside the river

almost all my pain

All that I have left now
is sand and ash in my hair

this knife

TALIESIN THINKS UPON HIMSELF

I am steel I am a druid
I am a poet I am a scientist
I am a serpent I am love
I am an apple still unbitten
I am the commanding bard
I am a stone floating in a lake
I am the rockwave sweeping the enemy away
I am the cell, the cleft, the restoration
I eat the octopus
I am a literary man
I am a tree lover stinking mad
fit to go drinking and thinking on art
I am an instrument in a thousand knots
I am the retinue of the army going to battle on my feet
I am shepherd of the district
I am ants on the heath
I lie unsheltered on the lichen, swearing in bloody thistles
I can reach the sky with my hook
I feed fish milk
I steal clothes from the naked
I spread butter on sand
I roof my house with feathers
Riches dissolve before me
I am chick of the chair!
Before I am dragged to my reward
Let me buy you a drink, Son of Mary!

BE LENIENT WITH ME

(tiny white signals
too small to be photographed)

I make no music
(exposed by the wind)

To spur the sorrow
(blue one I never meant to love)

the birds I have kept hidden in my attic
are quiet now

COMPASSION

She shook her fists as	Kamikaze embers
jumping roof to roof	fluttered overhead
Tusk of a dream left	Turkish girls
footprints in the butter	cajole the snakes
Unstoppable orbit pillows	mattresses beds springs
She touched the ground with tender	sweet sap running hot
Because I have loved so deeply	Because I have loved so deeply
Because I have loved so long	Because I have loved so long

SONG OF RAPES GONE BY

In a jagged place
where waves beat sand
after many a slaughter
soldiers broke my shores

They who fucked so loudly
in the end succumbed

I name them all enemy

My grave will be an island
all good daughters buried there

My grave will be deep
tall and narrow
the ground will hold me

And I will sleep
whatever monsters
the sea throws out
no new kings will penetrate
the borders of my death

GOODBYE BABY

my leaving will not touch you
rough little temper
good little captain
released between dark pillars
celebrated with tears and praise
entrusted to my hungry arms

(Thy large fountain fills the stream)

Deathsong ringing in my ear
I hear it perfectly

LAST WORDS IN THE DICTIONARY

little
past perfect tense

realm kingdom
forever always
loneliness aloneness solitude

darkness the gloom

they lie (bodily position)
people folks
ice
goldfinches

The appetites of tiny hands
folded knees
coltish in the yellow morning
it rains sadness
another word
released
furious virgin sex
among the clouds
emergency of giggling
drifting eyelids closed
before the flood
impenetrable
you are here with me
I will keep you here

ACCIDENTAL POEM BY CASEY

I see reality as it is
like I see you there, Mom
but then I like to upgrade
I think it could be better
if there were a city behind your ear
and there it is! And then
a rainbow on the other side

MORNING IN THE CHTHULUCENE

Chickadees scrap before the full roll of pleasure blinks eyelashes dreams sink into stomach turn spine legs head shake crack toes wiggle wiggle squeeze breasts heavy sore first day of a period stomach growls remember mother saying are you hungry? kids chuckle the little dog the one who warmed your back all night excites bites fingers stand and stretch one foot now two locate glasses lift the silver lid of computer from the wooden nightstand note white paint chipped at the corner screen alights on a mountain freckled with documents and you become historically situated

Acknowledgements

Noelle Allen helped conceive this project. At every obstacle, Noelle supported my work with integrity and compassion. I am very grateful to readers who responded to the manuscript at various stages including Jonathan Ball, Gary Barwin, Gregory Betts, Kate Marshall Flaherty, Jacob McArthur Mooney and Nikki Sheppy. My appreciation and thanks to the Ontario Arts Council for funding. To Jeremy Leipert, Cassius and Imogen Leipert, who I show everything, and ask relentlessly what I should do – thank you; I love you. To my family and friends, you are so beloved. I am so lucky to have this life with you.

Notes

In place of a hermeneutics we need an erotics of art. – Susan Sontag

Mummy, I made you a book because I love you! – Imogen

I wrote these poems as gifts that externalize the effects of other people's existence and their work on me and my work. This will be an ongoing practice. There were many influences I was unable to adequately capture. Several thinkers deeply influenced key parts of my thinking around the ethics of this project: Sara Ahmed's thinking about feminist living; Donna Haraway's concept of "tentacular thinking" about finding "kin" in the world, in animals and the environment, as well as with each other, to live and die together profoundly in an age that is not all about humanity. Haraway follows Hortense Spillers, who began talking about "kinship" and survival for Black women as early as 1985 in her "Review Essay: Kinship and Resemblances, Women on Women." Margaret Christakos coined the term "Influency," for her reading series where writers reflect at length on each others' work. I mention it here because influency articulates a way that reading and writing together become part of a fluent exchange outside of capitalist economies, part of a way of acknowledging that we make each other and that we must think about how to "be" together.

In most cases I gifted these poems to the people they were for in advance of publication and asked for permission for dedication. In some cases, across the process, I wrote poems that people said they did not want, and those poems were deleted from my hard drive – they will never exist in any form because that is not a good gift.

In the case of the poem that references the loss of Colten Boushie (though not by name), I received permission for the poem and this dedication / description from his mother, Debbie Baptiste. The poem's form was influenced by the work of Lillian Allen. That poem follows multiple written letters of protest to many institutions and is meant as an expression of ongoing support for the family.

The poem for Rehtaeh Parsons is my only ever illegal poem in that an earlier version was published on Twitter when it was illegal to publish her name.

In a very few cases – for example, Leonard Cohen and Taliesin – I was unable to obtain permission without a time machine, so it should be considered that those poems exist without permission (for now) – I can't say that is okay. In some cases, I am no longer in contact with people whose work I reflect on here – things change in charged times – but at the time of each poem's creation, I did notify those people and obtain their approval. For the sake of history, I did not want to erase those people or poems – I felt it best to still say how it was / who it was I considered. I hope that my intentions will be received as respectful, but they may not be. It's never a perfect process to be influenced by or to reference others or their work, and I accept criticism, even harsh criticism, as the right of all readers.

"Stages" is for Ronald Cummings.

"We" is for Jake Kennedy.

"We Camp above the Sea" is for Kaz Connelly.

"Instructions for the Wind:" is for Jonathan Ball.

"Let Us Compare Ecologies" is for Leonard Cohen.

"Wilderness Tips" and "Wildness" are for Erin Wunker – the photograph used for "Wildness" is of Pat Lowther.

"Perfectus Explicandum" is for Robin Richardson.

"Travel Light" is for Diana Fitzgerald Brydon.

"Sonnet for Sonnet" is for Sonnet L'Abbé.

"*It's plastic, Sachiko; keep it,* I said" is for Sachiko Murakami and angela rawlings.

"Motions of Confession" is for Nancy Dembowski.

"Packing for the Weekend" is for Natalie Zina Walschots.

"Summer Storm" is for Nicole Markotić.

"Mayhem Sonnet" and "Mayhem Remix" are for Tony Burgess.

"44 Things to Throw Away and Instantly Improve Your Life" is for Janet Leipert.

"By Design" is for Sachiko Murakami and first appeared as "Privilege" online at Project Rebuild (www.projectrebuild.ca).

"Response-ability" is for Gregory Scofield.

"They Will Take My Island" and "Symbols of Love or Trauma" are for Paul Vermeersch. "They Will Take My Island" first appeared online at *They Will Take My Island*: Paul Vermeersch's Arshile Gorky Project.

"I built a muscle" is for Nikki Reimer and Nathan Dueck.

"Echo Re-echo" is for Debbie Baptiste.

"Sandy" is for Sandy Pool.

"Grateful" is for Priscila Uppal.

"3,000" is for Harryette Mullen and Hoa Nguygen.

"And this is my first true speech" is for Amber Dawn and Lisa Robertson.

"Fireflies Stardust" is for Gerry Leipert.

"Let the Memory of Love Alone" is for Carole Lynn Stewart.

"'We only ever have one language.' Let us take it through one more round. Let us make it say what it does not know how to mean to say, and let us allow it to say something else." – Jacques Derrida, *Monolingualism of the Other*, trans. Patrick Mensah is for Nikki Sheppy.

"Love in the Chthulucene (Cthulhucene)" includes drawings and prints of rob mclennan, Weyman Chan, Helen Guri, kevin mcpherson eckhoff, Liz Howard, Sonnet L'Abbé, Ann Shin, Lillian Allen, Lucia Lorenzi and Klyde Broox, and it is for them and for Jessica Smith and Larissa Lai, who also influenced text and form. The image on page 78 is an eye miniature/Lover's Eye brooch by an unknown artist, c. 1790–1820, probably painted, oval-shaped frame set with twenty small pearls and two diamond "tears," Victoria & Albert Museum, London, https://collections.vam.ac.uk /item/O1067812/eye-miniature-unknown/.

"So Far" is for George Elliott Clarke in response to his response to me when he was Poet Laureate of Canada and I requested a poem as a citizen about the future.

"Children Are Figuratively Learning 'Cups' in Tears before the Talent Show" and "Let's Start All Over" are for Jacob McArthur Mooney.

"Beauty in Truth" is for Carmine Starnino.

"Life of Gary" is for Gary Barwin.

"Symbiopoesis" is for Gary Barwin and Gregory Betts.

"Taliesin Thinks upon Himself" is for Taliesin.

"Compassion" is for Jill Hartman.

"Last Words in the Dictionary" is for Erin Mouré and first appeared by permission of Elisa Sampedrín in *Open Letter* 14, no. 2 (Spring 2010).

"Accidental Poem by Casey" is for and by Cassius Leipert.

Trish Salah was inspirational in many ways although I did not have the confidence to make a poem for her (soon).

Selections of multiple poems have appeared in *The Calgary Renaissance*; in chapbook form, titled, *Love / Wildness* from above/ground press; on Lynn Crosbie's personal website; as part of The Pitch, a conversation with Carmine Starnino, in the *Partisan*, www.partisanmagazine.com/the-algonquin/2016/3/14 /eo2iq36j0z90z136olyh1m6djp1sti.

This is a picchur of Natalle caple

Natalee Caple is the author of nine books of poetry and fiction. Her work has been nominated for the KM Hunter Award, the RBC Bronwen Wallace Award, the Gerald Lampert Memorial Award, the ReLit Award and the Walter Scott Prize for Historical Fiction. Her latest novel, *In Calamity's Wake*, was published in Canada by HarperCollins and in the US by Bloomsbury. The novel in translation was published by Boréal and has been sold separately for publication in France. Natalee is an associate professor at Brock University.